LOYALTY, LEADERSHIP, AND THE PROFESSION: A GRASS ROOTS APPROACH TO CIVIL-MILITARY RELATIONS

As officers, you will have a responsibility to communicate to those below you that the American military must be non-political and recognize the obligation we owe the Congress to be honest and true in our reporting to them. Especially when it involves admitting mistakes or problems.

—Secretary Robert Gates at the 2007
U.S. Naval Academy Commencement

Civil-Military relations have become a hot topic among academics. Recently, with the "Revolt of the Generals," scholars have argued we are in a crisis with civil-military affairs that threatens our political process and our military readiness. Does a true problem really exist? Is this perceived tension between our uniformed leaders and our elected officials a new phenomenon?

Tension has always been there. Further, it is important for some level of tension to exist between our uniformed leaders and our elected officials. A respectful and engaged dialogue between civilian leaders and military professionals must exist. The Founding Fathers, framers of our Constitution, recognized the need for this engaged dialogue and wrote the Constitution to allow for constructive, creative tension between all branches of government. This includes our military leadership which falls under the executive branch and is funded by the legislative branch. As professionals, we must understand the foundations of our service and the underlying meaning of the oath we all take. Further, military professionals have to understand that if we create an environment that goes beyond creative tension to a situation in which trust is eroded between military professionals and elected leaders, we also erode the level of trust afforded us by the American people. Inherent in our Profession of Arms is the fundamental responsibility to earn and maintain the trust of the American people. As officers, we all have taken the oath of office by which we swear allegiance to the Constitution, and as such we enter into a relationship with civilian authority. This civilian - military relationship is at the core of our democratic system.

The idea of this tension in civil-military relations directly relates to our Profession of Arms, but first we must understand what "Profession of Arms" really means. Warfighters and elected officials inhabit different cultures; this fact contributes to the gap between them. This gap is especially relevant today because fewer members of Congress have served in the military. We must understand this clash of cultures and realize there are ethical dimensions in serving two masters. As people, we have choices. As professionals, we have fewer choices and this must be clearly understood as we manage this relationship.

The Theoretical Foundations of Civil-Military Relations

Before we can discuss culture, the responsibilities as related to our Profession of Arms and the underlying ethics, we must first understand the history of civil-military relationships. How is our system designed to operate and what are the pitfalls associated with this relationship becoming unbalanced?

The military's subordination to civilian control has been a key principle in our constitutional system since our nation was first founded. Our forefathers recognized that in a true democracy, there must first be stable governance and a defined process for electing officials accepted by the people as legitimate. In other words, the government must first be established and that government, elected by the people, should control all other state functions, including the military. The ratification of our Constitution established the responsibilities and roles of our President and Congress with regard to our military. Article I, section 8 of the Constitution grants Congress the power to declare war, raise and support an Army, and to provide and maintain a Navy. Article II, section 2 of the Constitution says, "the President shall be Commander in Chief of the Army and Navy of the United States." This clearly established military subordination to civilian authority. In his Pulitzer Prize winning book, *1776*, David McCullough illustrates this principle by describing General George Washington's resignation to Congress at the close of the Revolutionary War--an act that ensured his popularity as a national military leader would not overshadow the power of the fledgling Congress.[1] George Washington had enormous stature with the new nation and he used this and his political savvy to keep the Congress, the army, and the states focused on a common goal. When he disbanded the army after the war, he resolutely adhered to the principle of civilian control of the military.

The military profession has long recognized and embraced a tradition of service to country before self; this is evident in our oath when we swear to uphold the Constitution of the United States. The laws and regulations emanating from section 8 of the Constitution recognize the military's place in protecting freedom and vital national interests, while acknowledging the critical importance of balancing that role by placing it within the context of a constitutional democracy where the people, through their elected representatives, maintain ultimate authority over the government and the military.[2] The Founders recognized, and history has proven, that through this system the "blessings of liberty" are best secured. We therefore remain firmly grounded in the tenets of the Constitution. Civil-military relations are first set on basic principles, ideals, and a trust relationship with the American people. This trust relationship proves extremely important in guiding our actions and those of our elected leaders.[3]

The aforementioned trust relationship completes a critical triad affecting civil-military relations. A triangular set of relationships between the people, the government, and the military influences and defines the political and military aspects of our nation. The bonds of this relationship also influence our ability to defend our nation since an erosion of trust anywhere in the triad will result in destructive tension and weakness. In *On War*, Carl Von Clausewitz first alluded to this "trinity" when he wrote,

> The first of these three aspects mainly concerns the people; the second the commander and his army; the third the government. These three tendencies are like three different codes of law, deep-rooted in their subject and yet variable in their relationship to one another. To ignore any one of them would conflict with reality and be counter-productive. Our task therefore is to develop a relationship that maintains a balance between these three tendencies, like an object suspended between three magnets.[4]

Clausewitz used this trinity to explain his theory of war and the need for balance, but these relationships play a critical role in modern civil-military relations and the bonds of trust that the political and military circles enjoy with the nation.

War theorists have studied these critical relationships since the Treaty of Westphalia in 1648; they are essential in the political, military, and social processes of governance within our nation.[5] So why talk about these relationships outside the theory of war? Why is there need for balance in the context of civil-military relations? The answer is that these relationships are a matter of trust and that trust provides balance and stability within the system. The American people are responsible for electing our leaders and they trust them to make decisions and set policy in the best interests of the nation. The scope of these decisions is not limited to matters of the law but first extends to national security and the employment of our military. Citizens trust our civilian leaders to make sage decisions when blood and treasure are at stake. Since the military is comprised of their sons and daughters, the American people identify with our military leaders and have expectations regarding our character, loyalty, and ethics. The American people trust that we will honor the oath we take. They trust that we will meet their expectations for conduct, but most of all, they trust that we will exercise discipline, judgment, and loyalty as required by the Constitution which directs that we will serve our civilian masters. If the people witness excessive tension between civilian leaders and the military, they immediately become uncomfortable with the two great "arms" of our nation, each with its own currency.

We have seen evidence of politicalization of the military dating back to the Civil War. The modern military, however, reflects a level of politicalization that has renewed concerns. According to Samuel Huntington in *The Soldier and the State,* there is no clear break between civilians issuing orders and the military executing them.[6] Today, military and civilian leaders are tied together on policy and strategy matters like strands of the same rope. Because there is so much bilateral involvement, there is a natural erosion of trust and confidence with the people we serve when unhealthy tension exists between civilian and military leaders. This results in the nation having an uncomfortable lack of confidence in policy issues that affect national security and economic stability. In 2007, there was widespread, negative sentiment across the nation due to political and military disagreements over the 2007 U.S. troop surge in Iraq. The 24/7 news cycle and public statements made by civilian and military leaders led to national skepticism regarding what the proper course of action should be. In a two party system such as ours, the affect can be amplified. It would be prudent to divorce the military from politics, but globalization, expanding military roles, and political agendas driven by money and power have imbued the military with "Janus-like qualities." In *Common Defense,* Samuel Huntington focuses on the interaction between external and internal American military policy and the two faces of the military when he says, "the most distinctive, the most fascinating, and the most troublesome aspect of military policy is its Janus-like quality."[7] He contends that military policy not only faces in two directions, it exists in two worlds. One is international politics, the world of the balance of power, wars and alliances, the subtle and the brutal uses of force and diplomacy. The principal currency of this world is actual or potential military strength: battalions, weapons, and warships.[8] The other world is domestic politics, the world of interest groups, political parties, and social classes with their conflicting interests and goals. The currency here is the resources of society: men, money, and material.[9] Any major decision in military policy influences and is influenced by both worlds. A decision made in terms of one currency is always payable in the other. The rate of exchange, however, is usually in doubt.[10]

Huntington's writings reinforce the need for trust within this trinity called civil-military relations. Elected leaders must trust the military to execute policy as delineated by our National Command Authority and to provide sage, apolitical guidance to our civilian leaders. Military leaders must trust that our civilian masters understand our roles, missions and the consequences of military action when they employ us in any capacity. Lastly, the American people must completely trust that their elected government and the military will always put the needs and interests of the American people first. Unhealthy discord only serves to alert the people that there are conflicting ideals regarding their interests and the end result is a lack of confidence that can manifest itself in myriad ways that erode our leadership's legitimacy and effectiveness both at home and abroad.

Politicalization, Cultural Differences and Military Perspectives

Nations have engaged in combat to achieve political ends through military means. If Clausewitz was right when he said, "war is merely a continuation of politics by other means," can we ever truly divorce the military from politics and is there a need to do so? As I stated earlier, the politicalization of military officers continues to concern those who wish to safeguard the profession. In *The Future of the Army Profession,* Lloyd Matthews suggests that America's preeminent global role, the necessity to work closely with the governments of coalition partners, the increased role of joint military commands and agencies, as well as that of the press and the staffs and agencies of the Executive and the Congress, all argue that greater external involvement on the part of the military and its leaders will occur.[11] According to Matthews, there can be no doubt that military professionals of all ranks must develop more extensive political and cultural expertise if they are to effectively represent the profession in these proliferating interactions.[12]

The present military is a more professional and trusted organization than ever before. Average discretionary spending for defense is at an all-time high. As a result, the military has received increased publicity and become more transparent to the public. Today's battlefield is highly complex and civilian leaders have had to rely heavily on the advice, testimony and recommendations of military leaders. All this has garnered a level of popularity and support for the military among the American people that we have not seen in years past. The American public, probably in reaction to the lessons of Vietnam, has tremendous support for those in uniform. American society feels a social responsibility (which could also be labeled as "guilt") towards the military for enduring hardships that the vast majority of society has opted to avoid.[13] This level of support has not gone unnoticed in political circles. Elected and appointed politicians have aligned themselves with the military and often use the safety, welfare and support of our military and their families as a mantra for campaign speeches and economic platforms.

In light of all that has been written in recent years regarding a widening gap in civil-military relations, one could be alarmed given the complexity of global politics and military involvement around the world. I would argue that this "politicalization" is not the spectre of detrimental change. To the contrary, this is a necessary step in the evolution of our profession of arms. We should also remember that this is not a new phenomenon. Evidence of civil-military tension and politicalization in the U.S. dates back to at least the civil war.

The relationship between President Lincoln and General McClellan offers a classic case study in civil-military relations. General McClellan's self-confidence and military knowledge helped him gain promotion to his position as General-in-Chief, but ultimately, his arrogance and subtle disdain for Lincoln and his policies provided the catalyst for his demise.[14] Shortly after the Peninsula campaign which would bring the Army of the Potomac into Richmond, President Lincoln began to question McClellan's strategy and motives. Many believe McClellan had political aspirations fueled by his arrogance which caused him to question the President's grand strategy for winning the civil war-- the destruction of the Army of Northern Virginia. Historians such as Stephen

W. Sears believe that McClellan felt he could eventually take Richmond with little loss, which would increase his national popularity and facilitate a grand entrance into politics.[15] This tension between Lincoln and McClellan came to a head at Antietam in September of 1862. McClellan's refusal to pursue General Lee's Army and destroy it provoked Lincoln to relieve McClellan of his duties after the battle, prompted in part by the General's extreme aversion to risk in military strategy.[16] General McClellan would then run against President Lincoln in the elections of 1864 and lose.

The very public firing of General Douglas MacArthur by President Harry S. Truman on April 11, 1951 is also a good example. Truman relieved MacArthur from all his commands for publicly criticizing governmental policies in the Korean War. In his book, *Where the Buck Stops,* Truman wrote, "I fired MacArthur because he wouldn't respect the authority of the President. I didn't fire him because he was a dumb son of a bitch, although he was."[17] MacArthur received a hero's welcome home while Truman was widely scorned. The subsequent controversy created an enduring debate on the issue of civilian authority over the military, limited war versus total war, and the containment of communism. The dismissal of MacArthur by Truman created civil-military controversy which remains today.[18] In the context of civil-military relations, President Truman was right to fire MacArthur.

There were further struggles with civil-military relations during the war in Vietnam. In *Dereliction of Duty,* H.R. McMaster describes a house divided by interservice rivalries, a weak Joint Chiefs of Staff, and the hubris of President Johnson and his advisors. Tension resulted from the perception that military leaders knew how to win the war but were ignored by the political leadership.[19] Civil-military relations took

9

an interesting turn in the early nineties at the outset of the Clinton Administration. The administration cut defense spending as the U.S. cashed in on the post cold war "peace dividends." President Clinton also addressed policy concerning some controversial topics such as gays in the military. Clinton initiated the now-repealed Don't-Ask, Don't-Tell policy in 1993. These issues became very public. This publicized turmoil was a contemporary manifestation of longer-term systematic trends of division between top military and civilian leaders. Since Vietnam, the military has placed increased emphasis on political-military knowledge, leadership experience, and advanced education. At the same time, military experience among top civilian leaders declined due to the ending of the draft and public sentiment against the Vietnam War and the military.

The amalgamation of an increasingly politically savvy military and less military experience among political leaders will likely result in more military influence in the national security decision-making process. There has been a steady decline in military experience among senators and congressmen. Only 23 percent of the entire Congress has military experience compared to 68 percent back in 1991.[20] In 1993, civilian and military leadership ideals with regard to national security collided, which heightened civil-military tensions as military ideals prevailed.[21] The balance in civil-military affairs can be accomplished by continued focus on professionalization of the military as well as information exchange with newly elected civilian leaders. This can be accomplished through a variety of training and orientation methods much the same way we inform and train our newly promoted Brigadier Generals. The two must work closely together. Individual and personal relationships are the single most important factor in building effective civil-military relations and that starts with each understanding the other's role.

The military can, and should, embrace its increased need for political understanding. The growth of our military and preservation of our capabilities are crucial to national security efforts. In turn, this protects our global interests which directly affect our economic concerns and many other national issues. Military growth and continued professionalization will only occur with support from our elected officials and the country's electorate. In the eyes of the electorate, it becomes crucial that the military remain apolitical.

We have discussed civil-military tension and the military's increased political voice, but is the tension purely a by-product of the desire for power or is it something different? This tension is a simply matter of culture which, again, can be solved through education on both sides of the civil-military equation. The cultures which define and guide our civil and military leaders differ significantly. This difference requires both sides to continually remind themselves that this is not a competition but a relationship that supports the common good. We can look all the way back to George Washington's Presidential Farewell Address in which he warned that the nation and all men must move beyond partisanship in all aspects of government while remembering that the common good should be the focus of national leaders at all times.[22] This is not an argument for anything other than civilian control of the military but helps frame the problem so we, as professionals, can bring stability and balance to a complicated relationship that has a direct impact on strategy and policy in today's complex, global environment.

There should be no debating the fact that civilian control is fundamental to our process. According to Richard H. Kohn, civilian control allows a nation to base its values and purposes, its institutions and practices, on the popular will rather than on the choices of military leaders, whose outlook by definition focuses on the need for internal order and external security.[23] The highest values in a democratic society are freedom and civil liberty which directly clashes with a military culture that is based on martial customs and discipline. By definition, this makes the military an organization which is anything but democratic. Today's military culture enjoys more freedom than past generations but the institution still largely determines the scope of those freedoms. The military is designed to defend the nation through a centralized leadership structure that resembles a dictatorship.

In *An Essay on Civilian Control of the Military*, Kohn outlines the fundamental differences between civilian and military organizations. The military is fundamentally authoritarian while democratic society is consensual and participatory. We have an all-volunteer force and we knowingly sacrifice some consensual choices when we enter service. This concept is essential in the framework of military operations to ensure a strict chain of command is followed to facilitate the execution of military operations. Military orders cannot be carried out on a participatory basis.[24]

The military is hierarchical and society is essentially egalitarian. For the military to function, there must be a strict hierarchy for issuing and following orders. This hierarchical framework also supports the virtue of discipline which is vital to military organizations. By contrast, civil society places people on an equal plane and fundamentally seeks an equal voice and representation from everyone. The military could not operate in this manner.[25]

The military insists on discipline and obedience, subordinating personal needs and desires to the group and to a mission or goal. American society is individualistic, attempting to achieve the greatest good for the largest number by encouraging the pursuit of individual needs and desires in the marketplace and in personal lives, each person relying upon their own talents and ingenuity.[26] Structure, order, conformity and homogeneity are all characteristics of the military organization while society tolerates, even celebrates, disagreement and diversity of perspective.[27] The military could never tolerate levels of disagreement and individuality that would endanger our wartime mission or the lives of our most precious resource: Soldiers, Sailors, Airmen, and Marines. The military culture demands discipline and an underlying ethos that places the safety and security of the team and the institution second only to the defense of the nation. This breeds a culture of selfless service among our military members to protect the nation.

Civilian leaders, by contrast, share different motivations and exude a different type of discipline or commitment to their organizations. As an example, most Marines and Soldiers share a sense of espirit de corps and connection with their respective institutions that we do not see in Congress. Elected leaders have a sense of loyalty to their states and constituents but it is different than what we see in military organizations. Elected leaders are driven by political affiliations and the desires of their constituents yet they share a fundamental desire to protect the republic as a whole. I would argue, however, that their loyalty to a "whole of government" approach that favors selfless service to the nation is often overshadowed by partisanship and political agendas;

therein lies one source of tension and the erosion of trust between civilian and military leaders.

The perception that a general skepticism and distrust exists between civilian and military leaders is an unpopular viewpoint that few want to address, yet the perceptions are real. For example, I posed the same question to 50 civilians and 50 military members represented by all four services: "Do you think there is tension between civilian and military leadership and what do you view as the primary catalyst?" Ninety-five percent felt that there are always tensions that ebb and flow between healthy and unhealthy. The civilian group favored military opinions over those offered by civilian leadership on matters of national security and foreign policy. Many also felt that elected officials do not represent the people as a whole. This response echoes a recent nationwide Rasmussen Poll which found that when it comes to important national issues, 73% of adults nationwide trust the judgment of the American people more than that of America's political leaders. Understanding that the American people do not equal military leadership, this is clear evidence that the nation does not feel represented by their elected officials.[28] During my questioning, over 75% of all surveyed felt that partisanship, political agendas, and corruption among civilian leaders resulted in an erosion of trust with the American people and military leadership. Most military members reported that their first inclination is to question political motives when dealing with political leadership.

Speculation suggests that the average American citizen's ideals, character, and foundational values are more in line with those shared by military members which is a disturbing trend since our elected officials are supposed to represent the ideals and desires of the people who elected them. Although political corruption and partisan friction tarnish these trust relationships, many civilian leaders share a tireless, deep devotion to the republic, democracy, and the American people; understanding this is an essential part of educating the military side of the civil-military equation.

Despite these cultural differences, Dr. Don Snider, a recognized expert in civil-military relationships, believes the two sides can find middle ground "where equal dialogue and unequal authority reside."[29] Regardless of perception, the military has no purpose but to serve the American people and the Constitution, which in turn means they serve their elected officials and appointed representatives. In all aspects of its existence and operations, the Profession of Arms should advise with disciplined candor and remain willingly subordinate to, and a servant of, civilian authorities.[30] Further, members of the Profession of Arms clearly understand and accept the subordination of their personal needs to the needs of the greater good. According to Richard Kohn, the point of civilian control is to make security subordinate to the larger purposes of a nation, rather than the other way around. The purpose of the military is to defend society, not to define it. While a country may have civilian control of the military without democracy, it cannot have democracy without civilian control.[31]

Serving Two Masters: A Challenge of Ethics or Loyalty?

We have discussed the theoretical foundations which guide our actions as military professionals and built upon those foundations with a discussion surrounding the bonds of trust shared with a nation. The next step is to analyze the moral imperative faced by military leaders in our service to our political leaders and our citizens. For the purposes of this discussion, service to our citizens will also encompass the responsibilities we have to our service members. There is most certainly an ethical dimension in the service of both masters but this internal dilemma is often times easily resolved depending on the nature of the ethical or moral principle in question. As warfighters, we have all been given orders and asked the question, "why?" or "is there a better way?" but at the tactical and operational level, these conflicts are usually easily remedied and we carry-on smartly. Certainly there have been examples in our history such as the My Lai massacre or Abu Ghraib but these isolated incidents are extreme and the breeches in ethics, morals, and basic human decency are clear in such cases. As military professionals, we follow orders and although we have the freedom to voice concerns and propose alternate courses of action, the end result is that we follow the lawful decisions of our superiors.

The issues of ethics and loyalty are more difficult at the strategic and national level where they are key to the decision-making process. This is the nexus of decision points between political and military leaders. Civil-military tension lives here. Is this tension due to conflict over ethical and moral issues or is it simply an issue of loyalty? Our civilian leaders do not intentionally seek options that will harm our country or its institutions or that might cause needless bloodshed. Though driven by political agendas, they understand the tremendous burden they bear in committing our sons and daughters in the defense of our nation. Their decisions do not necessarily violate basic moral principles or ethical guidelines so the tension is not merely an issue of ethics. Military professionals feel a deep, unwavering loyalty to our citizens, our service-members and the institution.

Politicians are loyal to their parties and the basic ideology and rhetoric that will keep them in office so they can continue to affect policy at the macro level. Senior military leaders have a different loyalty. Their loyalty is to the rich traditions of a

timeless profession and the nation they serve and protect. They start at the lowest

levels of their service and methodically work their way up while building valuable

experience and expertise. They become emotionally and personally attached to making

the institution better and to the brave souls they lead.

In 2006, several retired General Officers made public statements regarding the

political leadership of our country and our failed strategy in Iraq. This event became

known as the "Revolt of the Generals." Although the "Revolt of the Generals" was a

highly criticized event by many scholars, it provides evidence that there are perceived

differences in culture and loyalty between our military leaders and politicians. In an

address to military reporters and editors in 2003, Lieutenant General(ret) Ricardo

Sanchez stated,

> Since 2003, the politics of war have been characterized by partisanship as the Republican and Democratic parties struggled for power in Washington. At times, these partisan struggles have led to political decisions that endangered the lives of our sons and daughters on the battlefield. The unmistakable message was that political power has greater priority than our national security objectives.[32]

In a senior leader panel at the Foreign Policy Research Institute, Marine Corps

Lieutenant General(ret) Gregory Newbold further demonstrated this loyalty to the

institution and those who serve when he said that our young men and women deserve

ethical and loyal leaders who will represent those who stand to make the ultimate

sacrifice and have no voice.[33] Both men were severely criticized for their open remarks

regarding the political leaders in Washington and both men's comments have ethical

undertones, but it is loyalty to their profession and the men and women in their charge

that provided the impetus for their comments.

If culture matters and the tensions that exist between civilian and military leaders are more an issue of loyalty, then how do we address the problem and who bears the responsibility to fix it? Based on the tenets of our military profession, our responsibilities to the country and the people, and our ability to operate in both the military and political realms, senior military leaders should bear the burden of navigating the civil-military relationship by ensuring that the common good remains the focal point. A senior military officer can operate more effectively on both sides of the relationship as opposed to a career politician who can operate effectively on the political side but not necessarily the military side. This is not an indictment of character but one of credibility. The simple truth is that the military side of that equation identifies deeply with those who share the same culture and loyalties.

Senior military leaders have risen to their current positions because, in theory, they are strong leaders, persuasive negotiators, charismatic speakers, and team builders. By the time one becomes a Colonel or General, he or she should be able to interact effectively with civilian leaders. Politicalization of the military is a sign of the times and today's senior leaders must be able to navigate and operate in a political environment. Snider argues that senior military leaders must understand the art of politics. Although they operate in a political arena, the senior military leader is not *part* of that arena. The senior military leader is not a politician and should remain resolutely nonpartisan, yet he must understand what makes a politician tick, such as the give and take, the rhythms of political life and the art of negotiation.[34] I think senior military leaders and politicians with military experience better understand the human toll and therefore bear the mantle of responsibility to "get it right" for the country. Senior military leaders also understand that civilian control of the military should not be disputed and they have the added responsibility of knowing when negotiation is over and obedience to orders begins.

In civil-military relationships, personalities matter and there will always be some level of tension. Tension can be good if focused in a way that encourages open, constructive dialogue for the purposes of national interests. This means that both political and military leaders share responsibility for "making things work." This is not magic. Personalities and interests define the environment. Education, character, compromise, and selfless service are the tools that both sides must use to navigate the environment. The focus on ethics and the profession that we currently teach at all senior professional military education colleges has made a tremendous difference in the way senior military and political leaders interact with each other.

The Role of Dissent

One last aspect of this relationship must be discussed: the idea of dissent. What is dissent? Simply defined, "dissent" means "to differ in opinion." Certainly, considering all opinions is not a bad thing when we are talking about decisions involving the future of our great nation. In its purest form, dissent is healthy within the civil-military relationship as long as everyone knows its limits and recognizes the military is still subordinate to civilian leadership. Dissent only becomes a corrosive and divisive tool when either party allows it to become public for the purposes of undermining the other. The "Revolt of the Generals" again illustrates the difference. The generals have faced both criticism and praise for speaking out against the Iraq war and failed military policies and strategy. Is it ever okay to publicly dissent if you are serving or have ever served in the military? A discussion of loyalty sheds light on the question.

Lieutenant General(ret) Gregory Newbold is an inherently private person whose record of military service and commitment to his Marines and our nation is unquestioned. Lieutenant General(ret) Newbold does not question civilian control of the military. He believes that uniformed strategic leaders should obey to the very limits of their professional tolerance and that "Uniforms" should resist speaking out publicly against their leaders. However, he also believes that every professional must cross the line if the situation becomes egregious.[35] So what prompted him to speak out against the U.S. involvement in Iraq?

In a March 2004 interview on ABC News, John McWethy asked Secretary Rumsfeld, "Now, a year after the war began, thousands of Iraqis and more than 585 Americans are dead. How are we to view the steady stream of body-bags coming back from Iraq – of American troops?"[36] Secretary Rumsfeld replied, "Every person who is killed or wounded is a heartbreak. Certainly for me and for their families and for their loved ones. In the case of this conflict, every single person is a volunteer. Every person there put their hand up and said, send me. I want to participate in the defense of our country."[37] In Lieutenant General(ret) Newbold's heart, this comment crossed the line and the passion and loyalty he felt for every Soldier, Sailor, Airmen, and Marine brought him to the decision to publicly discuss his thoughts, after he retired.

Lieutenant General(ret) Newbold has declared that public dissent while *in uniform* is not acceptable and should not be considered. The downstream costs of public dissent while in uniform would be an erosion of the vital trust relationships. The immediate public reaction would be to question the commitment and credibility of both military and civilian leadership. In *Dissent and Strategic Leadership of the Military*

Profession, Snider recognizes that public dissent will reverberate outward, impinging at a minimum on three critical trust relationships of the military profession—those with the American people, those with civilian and military leaders at the highest levels of decision-making, and those with the junior corps of officers and noncommissioned officers of our armed forces.[38]

If certain types of public dissent while in uniform are not an option, then what are the limits? While in uniform, I believe there are two acceptable forms of dissent. The first is candid, honest testimony before Congress that should include personal opinion if asked. The second is resignation. When testifying before Congress, military leaders have a solemn obligation to answer questions with candor. As stated, we serve our political masters and when asked, our service-members, citizens, and political leadership deserve the frank benefits of our experience and expertise. I believe there is a place for professional opinion in this case and not just the public position of the military chain of command.

The second acceptable form of dissent while in uniform is resignation. Resignation--as contrasted with retirement--includes forfeiture of all pay and benefits. In the eyes of our political masters, resignation of senior military officers sends a clear message but it does so in a "not-so-public forum." If you have reached that subjective limit where further service is in direct violation of personal ethics and loyalty to those you serve, then your choice is clear and further service would do nothing more than undermine the credibility of your convictions. Lieutenant General(ret) Newbold recognized this when he said,

> I regret that I did not speak more openly to our civilian leaders. Flaws in
> our civilians are one thing; the failure of the Pentagon's military leaders is

quite another. Those are men who know the hard consequences of war but, with few exceptions, acted timidly when their voices urgently needed to be heard.[39]

Lieutenant General(ret) Newbold thought many military leaders felt the same way he did yet said nothing, and to him, this was a violation of the quintessential moral imperative.

What are the limits of dissent for retired officers? Are we bound to the same code of ethics and service that guide us in uniform? For the generals who revolted, the answer is obviously, "no." Does this type of dissent have the same affects as uniformed dissent on the trust relationships with those we serve? Public dissent when out of uniform has its place if done in the proper manner. If we leave military service and have opinions that could save the lives of our young men and women or uncover egregious acts and inept leadership, don't we have a responsibility to speak? We are dealing with people on both sides of the civil-military relationship and people are subject to mistakes and errors in judgment. This type of dissent does not affect the trust relationships in the same way because by virtue of timing, these discussions center on past issues and not those in the present and that places them under a different lens with the nation.

The last thing to consider here is the matter of motivation. What motivates an officer to publicly dissent? Although I have pointed out several examples from history, the circumstances are truly extraordinary for senior military officers to publicly dissent. Motivation often determines acts of authentic and genuine leadership versus self-serving acts for political gain or otherwise. I have no doubts about the genuine, loyal, and heartfelt nature of comments made by Lieutenant Generals Newbold, Zinni, and Sanchez. By contrast, many believe that comments made by General Wesley Clark were politically motivated and self-serving. General Wesley Clark told anchor Tim

Russert that Bush administration officials had engaged in a campaign to implicate Saddam Hussein in the September 11 attacks. Clark said that he had been called on September 11 and urged to link Baghdad to the terror attacks.[40] Further, he openly aligned himself with a political party which immediately calls into question his motivations.

Is there any good that comes from public dissent by military officers? In theory, there are rare cases in which public dissent has had positive effects on the civil-military relationship as well as the trust relationships that we have discussed. When the "Revolt of the Generals" occurred, many believed there was a widening gap in civil-military affairs that threatened the good order and discipline of the armed forces as well as our political process. Since 2006, the revolt, along with every article and interview by the Generals, has been discussed in detail at formal military schools. Most notably, dissent, the profession, and civil-military affairs receive a great deal of focus at our senior military colleges where we educate the strategic thinkers and leaders of tomorrow. Although perceived as a crisis at the time, the actions by those senior officers brought attention to weak areas in civil-military affairs that have been strengthened through education and scholarly discussion. We can look to history and say the same thing for every incident that has occurred from Lincoln and McClellan, to Truman and MacArthur, and Rumsfeld and the Generals.

Conclusion

Much has been written on the subject and causes of Civil-Military tension and the concept of civilian control of the military. The tenets of our "Profession of Arms" play an important role at the nexus of political and military leadership. Senior military professionals must understand that there is a political nature to our profession that must be understood and applied to help us navigate civil-military relationships. Military culture reinforces resolute loyalty in officers. However, this is also where education, strategic leadership, and critical thinking are truly put to the test. These tools are at our disposal to shape these relationships. Public dissent is not an option nor an obligation. Private dissent has its place but can be destructive to trust relationships and our profession if undertaken in the wrong manner. Our obligation is to the American people, our profession, and to our civilian leaders. Resident in that obligation is honesty and courage in communicating to our leaders.

Further, our civilian leaders need to encourage and embrace an open dialogue that is constructive and professional. This very basic principle has been a bedrock of success for many great leaders in our nation's history. Political imperatives should never outweigh military effectiveness and political and military end-states should never be mutually exclusive, for this is where true tension arises in civil-military affairs. As military leaders, we have an obligation to voice our concerns to our leaders. Actions that erode the civil-military relationship serve only to undermine our mission and the trust relationship with the American people.

Endnotes

[1] David McCullough, *1776* (New York, NY: Simon and Schuster, 2005), 292-294.

[2] Army Combined Arms Center of Excellence for the Professional Military Ethic,"Information Paper of American Civil-Military Relations," https://www.us.army.mil/suite/page/611545 (June 28, 2010).

[3] Ibid.

[4] Carl Von Clausewitz, *On War* (Princeton, NJ: Princeton University Press, 1976), 89.

[5] Army Combined Arms Center of Excellence for the Professional Military Ethic,"Information Paper of American Civil-Military Relations," https://www.us.army.mil/suite/page/611545 (June 28, 2010).

[6] Samuel P. Huntington, *The Soldier and the State: The Theory and Politics of Civil Military Relations*(Cambridge, MA: Belknap Press, 1957), 352.

[7] Samuel P. Huntington, *The Common Defense: Strategic Programs in National Politics* (New York: Columbia University Press, 1961), 1.

[8] Ibid.

[9] Ibid.

[10] Samuel P. Huntington, *The Common Defense: Strategic Programs in National Politics* (New York: Columbia University Press, 1961), 1.

[11] Mathews, Lloyd J., ed. *The Future of the Army Profession.* Don M. Snider, Project Director. 2nd ed. (Boston, MA: McGraw-Hill, 2005), 625.

[12] Ibid.

[13] Wong, Leonard. *Colloquium Brief.* Harvard Kennedy School, Web. 16 Feb. 2010. <www.StrategicStudiesInstitut.army.mil. >.

[14] Dallas Woodrum, "Lincoln and McClellan," The Cellar: Utraque Unum, (October 2007): 53-57.

[15] Stephen W. Sears, *George B. McClellen: The Young Napoleon*, (New York, NY: Ticknor and Fields, 1988), 344.

[16] Ibid.

[17] Harry S. Truman, *Where the Buck Stops*, (Warner Books, 1989), 214.

[18] Robert J. Donovan, *Conflict and Crisis: The MacArthur-Truman Controversy*, University of Missouri; First edition (April 1, 1996)

[19] H.R. McMaster, *Dereliction of Duty* (New York, NY: HarperCollins Publishers, 1997), 87

[20] Military Officer's Association of America, "Declining Military Experience in Congress," January 2011, http://www.moaa.org/lac/lac_resources/lac_resources_tips/ lac_resources_tips_decline.htm (accessed February 8, 2011).

[21] Gibson, Christopher P; Snider, Don M., *Civil-Military Relations and the Potential to Influence: A Look at the National Security Decision-Making Process,* Armed Forces and Society, volume 25, issue 2, April 1999

[22] Washington, George. *George Washington's Farewell Address*, (Bedford, MA: Applewood Books, 1999) 24.

[23] Kohn, Richard H., "An Essay on Civilian Control of the Military," 1997, http://www.unc.edu/depts/diplomat/AD_Issues/amdipl_3/kohn.html (accessed February 13, 2011)

[24] Ibid.

[25] Ibid.

[26] Ibid.

[27] Ibid.

[28] Rasmussen Reports, "73% Trust Judgment of People More Than Politicians." 2009, http://www.rasmussenreports.com/public_content/politics/general_politics/february_2009/73_trust_judgment_of_people_more_than_politicians (accessed February 28, 2011)

[29] Snider, Don M., Nielsen, Suzanne C., *American Civil-Military Relations: The Soldier and the State in a New Era* (Baltimore, MD: The Johns Hopkins University Press, 2009), 293.

[30] U.S. Army TRADOC, *An Army White Paper: The Profession of Arms.* CG TRADOC Approved, 8 Dec 2010. 8.

[31] Kohn, Richard H., "How Democracies Control the Military," *Journal of Democracy* 8, no. 4 (October 1997) 150.

[32] LTG(ret) Ricardo Sanchez, "Civil-Military Affairs," address, Luncheon, Washington, DC, October 12, 2007, public record.

[33] LTG(ret) Gregory Newbold, "Mind the Gap: Post Iraq Civil-Military Relations in America," lecture, Foreign Policy Research Institute, Washington, DC, October 15, 2007, public record.

[34] Snider, Don M., Nielsen, Suzanne C., *American Civil-Military Relations: The Soldier and the State in a New Era* (Baltimore, MD: The Johns Hopkins University Press, 2009), 65-66.

[35] LTG(ret) Gregory Newbold, "Mind the Gap: Post Iraq Civil-Military Relations in America," lecture, Foreign Policy Research Institute, Washington, DC, October 15, 2007, public record.

[36] John McWethy, "Primetime, ABC News," interview, Washington, DC, March 25, 2004, public record.

[37] Secretary Donald H. Rumsefeld, "Primetime, ABC News," interview, Washington, DC, March 25, 2004, public record.

[38] Snider, Don M. *Dissent and Strategic Leadership of the Military Professions.* Carlisle Barracks, PA: US Army War College, Strategic Studies Institute, February 2008. 7.

[39] LTG Gregory Newbold, "Why Iraq Was a Mistake," Time Magazine (April 9, 2006): 4.

[40] FAIR:Fairness and Accuracy in Reporting, "Media Silent on Clark's 9/11 Comments," June 2003, http://www.fair.org/index.php?page=1842(accessed February 14, 2011).